T0346816

SEAGULL SEAGULL

Selected poems from THE TREE HOUSE

James K. Baxter

Illustrations by Kieran Rynhart

GECKO PRESS

THE GRASSHOPPER

Grasshopper green,
Grasshopper grey,
Why do you sit and fiddle all day?

Grasshopper grey,
Grasshopper green,
Tell me the wonderful things that you've seen.

CONTENTS

THE TREE HOUSE

John and Judith
And Billy and me,
We have our own house
In a willow tree.

It's built of boards
And battens and tin
From the packing case
That the tractor came in.

Up the slippery trunk
Of the tree we climb
With a rope to help us,
One at a time;

But once we're up
And safe inside
Only the wind knows
Where we hide.

Down in the paddock
The brown horse neighs
And in stormy weather
The whole house sways

Like a ship at sea
While the branches roar
And birds fly past
At the open door.

RAIN

When I go walking
Out in town
I lift my umbrella
As the rain comes down.

I pull on my gumboots
And I button up my coat;
When the gutter's like a river
I play there with my boat.

Though the cats run inside
And the little dogs huddle,
I go splash, splash,
Through the biggest puddle.

Till over the hill
Flies the rain and the storm,
And I open my coat
As the sun shines warm.

SWING, SWING, SWING

Swing, swing, swing,
Swinging wide and high –
If you swing high enough
Your feet will touch the sky.

If your foot should touch it
Then the sky will break.
It'll make no difference when you say
You did it by mistake.

The sun will growl and grumble,
The stars will tumble down,
And the weather Man come running
In a long, black gown.

The rivers will run backwards,
The sums will add up wrong;
You'll come to school on Saturday
And play the whole night long.

It will take a ton of thistledown,
A ladder brought from Spain,
And a new magician's hammer
To patch it up again.

TWENTY LITTLE ENGINES

Twenty little engines
Whistling in the yard –
One lost his whistle
And he cried SO hard

That every little engine
STOPPED in the yard
And the stationmaster ran
And BELLOWED to the guard,

'Tommy's lost his whistle,
His long, loud whistle,
And no one can shunt
When he's crying so hard.'

The guard said, 'WHAT?'
And the guard said, 'WHO?
I've a brand new whistle
That I think will do;

'It's made of copper
And it's made of tin;
There's a hole at the bottom
Where the steam goes in;

'There's a hole at the top
Where the steam goes out,
Just like the whistle
On a tea kettle spout.

'It goes – *Peep! Peep!*
And it goes – *Hoo! Hoo!*
It's just the kind of whistle
That will do for you.'

Twenty little engines
Shunting in the sun –
Tommy got his whistle
And the work WAS DONE.

ANDY DANDY

Andy Dandy Ne'er-do-well
Made his hat from a coconut shell,
With a bamboo pipe and a jacket of straw
And a cucumber house with a bell at the door.
'If you want to come in, just ring the bell,'
Said Andy Dandy Ne'er-do-well.

JACK FROST

Look out, look out,
Jack Frost's about!
He'll nip your ears
And bite your snout!

He'll chap your knees
And make you sneeze;
Your fingers and
Your toes he'll freeze.

His magic makes
The mountains grow;
He learnt it from
His mother, Snow.

Yet he makes tiny
Glittering fronds
On window panes,
And ice on ponds.

When out of school
We dance and skip
He's waiting there
To pinch and nip.

Beware! Beware!
Leave nothing bare
When Jack Frost whistles
Through the air.

IF I WERE KING OF SWEDEN

If I were King of Sweden
I would never wear a crown,
But I'd ride in a golden carriage
With the window down.

I would wake up very early
In my palace by the sea;
I would breakfast on marshmallow
And have the same for tea.

Each day would be my birthday,
I'd buy fizzy drink in kegs;
Once a month there'd be an Easter
With enormous Easter eggs.

If I saw a man or woman
Who looked hungry in the street,
I'd invite them in to dinner
And give them pies to eat.

If I were King of Sweden
I'd go walking to and fro,
And every person that I met
Would stop and say, 'Hullo!'

THE SNOWMAN

Out in the garden
The snowman stands
With his black button eyes
And twigs for hands,

With his old torn hat
And his floor-mop hair.
He hasn't even
A coat to wear.

He likes the winter
And the sparrows that come
To perch on his shoulder
When their toes are numb.

The wind blows north
And the wind blows south,
But he stands and grins
With a pipe in his mouth.

Whichever way
The wind may blow,
He does not mind
The frost and snow.

But when daffodils flutter
On a fine spring day
He'll dribble and squelch
And melt away,

And the sparrows will find
Next day at dawn
A little grey heap
On the garden lawn.

THE GROWLY BEAR

The growly bear,
The growly bear,
He lives in the cupboard
Under the stair.

His hat and his boots
And his breeches are brown,
And he sleeps all day
On a brown eiderdown.

At night he goes walking
About by himself
To gobble up the honey
On the kitchen shelf.

You can hear him growling
Wherever he goes,
But just what he looks like
Nobody knows.

THE GORSE FIRE

Oh what a worry
When the gorse bushes catch!
Somebody careless
Has dropped a match.

Somebody careless
Let it fall down,
Took no notice
That the grass was brown.

A little thin flame
Came galloping fast
Then roared up higher
Than the top of a mast.

The black smoke climbed
Like a tower in the sky
Till there was no room
For the birds to fly,

And the crackling bushes
Blazed higher and higher
Up the brown hillside
Like a river on fire!

THE SEAGULL

'Seagull, seagull,
Riding high,
What do you see
With your bold, bright eye?'

'I see the sun
On a winter morning
Over the edge
Of the broad sea burning;

'I see the boats
On the harbour smoking;
I see an engine
With the stoker stoking.

'I see the town
And a church with its steeple,
And the pavements full
Of hurrying people.

'The men and women
And girls and boys
Look far, far smaller
Than painted toys.

'I like to glide
On my wings and stare
I like to ride
On the pillowy air;

'But if you'll throw me
A crust or two,
I'll come right down
And eat with you.'

THE SHEPHERD

Where rivers tumble
In gorges deep,
High on the mountain
I muster sheep –

The scraggy, wild ewe
That has never been shorn
And the big, rough ram
With his curly horn.

The sun shines down
Like a burning-glass
As they nibble the fresh, green
Tussock grass.

The tracks they make
With their nimble toes
No one but me
And my old dog knows.

With a long, low whistle
I send him out.
He cocks his ears
To hear me shout.

He is tired and dusty
Before the night –
His tongue hangs dripping
And his teeth gleam white.

When the cold stars glitter
And my door is shut,
We sit by the fire
In our mountain hut.

EEL FISHING

Sunlight and floating seeds
On the black surface of the water hole
At the river's elbow, where great eels
Bask on a mud bottom,
And manuka branches from the high bank
Roof the river over.

All at once among the rushes
Two boys come running, splashing,
With bare feet and old clothes,
With eyes brighter than a bird's,
With catgut, hooks, and line,
With quick shouts and silence.
They climb to a branch of the oldest tree
And drop their lines into the bog-black water.

THE SHIPS

The little ships
From the harbour sail
Bang in the teeth
Of a southerly gale.

The great white waves
Wash to and fro:
Drum, drum, drum,
Say the engines below.

With their oilskins on
The captains stand;
They drop their nets
Far out from land.

And they bring home,
For you and me,
Snapper and groper
And tarakihi.

Then the little ships
At anchor lie,
And the captains' coats
Hang up to dry.

THE BIG BLACK WHALE

I wish I were a big, black whale
Out in the deep green sea.
He blows like a hose
Through the top of his nose,
As happy as a whale can be,
And the sailors look pale
When they hear his tail
Go smack, smack, smack,
On a big wave's back
Out in the deep green sea.

SPRING-HEELED JACK

Spring-heeled Jack
Jumped up and down
Higher than anyone
Else in the town.

The heels of his boots
Were fitted with springs;
He could fly
Like a bird with wings.

The first time up
He jumped so high
He made thunder
In the sky.

The second time up
He jumped far higher –
The North Wind set
His coat on fire.

The third time up
He jumped with zest –
The eagles plucked
His hair for a nest.

But the very last time
Spring-heeled Jack
Jumped to the moon
And never came back.

OLD MAN JEREMY

Old man Jeremy
Had a boat.
He went for a row
In his overcoat.

But the wind went round
And round about
Till the overcoat
Blew inside out.

Old man Jeremy
Swam to the shore.
He never went
For a row any more.

THE SKINDIVER

Drifting, drifting under sea,
I had no sins
But only fins;
My aqualung
Did not go bung;
Fish learnt to fear
My clever spear;
I swam with skill
Until, until
A Cook Strait squid got hold of me.

THE OLD OWL

'Tu whit! Tu whoo!'
The old owl said –
'Pack your toys
And get ready for bed.

'As I sit on the branch
Of a grey gum tree
There's nobody here
But the moon and me;

'There's nobody here
But me and the moon,
And I'll go a-hunting
For my supper soon.

'A beetle, a bug
And a brown field mouse,
I'll bring them home
To my gum tree house.

'I'm old as old,
And wise as wise,
And I see in the dark
With my great round eyes.

'So hurry and scurry,'
The old owl said –
'Pack your toys
And get ready for bed.'

This selection first published in 2020 by Gecko Press
PO Box 9335, Wellington 6141, New Zealand
info@geckopress.com

Poems © James K. Baxter Trust 2020
Illustrations © Kieran Rynhart 2020
© Gecko Press Ltd 2020

The Tree House and Other Poems for Children was first published by Price Milburn, 1974

'The Skindiver' first published in *A Selection of Poetry* (Poetry magazine, 1964)

All rights reserved. No part of this publication may be reproduced or transmitted or utilized in any form, or by any means, electronic, mechanical, photocopying or otherwise without the prior written permission of the publisher.

Gecko Press acknowledges the generous support of Creative New Zealand

Design and typesetting by Vida Kelly
Printed in China by Everbest Printing Co. Ltd, an accredited ISO 14001 & FSC-certified printer

ISBN 978-1-776572-81-6

For more curiously good books, visit geckopress.com